About the Author™

Meet

Lois Lowry

Frances E. Ruffin

The Rosen Publishing Group's
PowerKids Press™
New York

For Lorna Choisy, our dear family friend and great lover of books

Published in 2006 by The Rosen Publishing Group, Inc.
29 East 21st Street, New York, NY 10010

First Edition

Editor: Rachel O'Connor
Layout Design: Julio A. Gil

Photo Credits: All photos courtesy of Lois Lowry.

Grateful acknowledgement is made for permission to reprint previously published material:
p. 6 From ANASTASIA KRUPNIK by Lois Lowry. Copyright © 1979 by Lois Lowry. Reproduced by permission of Houghton Mifflin Company. All rights reserved.
p. 10 From THE GIVER by Lois Lowry. Copyright © 1999 by Lois Lowry. Reproduced by permission of Houghton Mifflin Company. All rights reserved.
p. 14 From NUMBER THE STARS by Lois Lowry. Copyright © 1989 by Lois Lowry. Reproduced by permission of Houghton Mifflin Company. All rights reserved.
p. 17 (top right) "Jacket Cover" from ANASTASIA KRUPNIK by Lois Lowry. Used by permission of Random House Children's Books, a division of Random House, Inc.
p. 19 (inset) From NUMBER THE STARS (JACKET COVER) by Lois Lowry. Used by permission of Random House Children's Books, a division of Random House, Inc.

Library of Congress Cataloging-in-Publication Data

Ruffin, Frances E.
  Meet Lois Lowry / Frances E. Ruffin.
     p. cm. — (About the author)
  Includes bibliographical references and index.
  ISBN 1-4042-3129-3 (library binding)
  1. Lowry, Lois—Juvenile literature. 2. Authors, American—20th century—Biography—Juvenile literature. 3. Children's stories—Authorship—Juvenile literature. I. Title. II. Series.

  PS3562.O923Z85 2006
  813'.6—dc22

                                    2004025406

Manufactured in the United States of America

Contents

1 A Life in Fiction   5

2 The Middle Child   6

3 A Childhood in Carlisle   9

4 Life in Tokyo   10

5 Marriage and a Family   13

6 First Children's Book   14

7 Making Life Changes   17

8 The Highest Award   18

9 A Writer's Life   21

10 In Her Own Words   22

Glossary   23

Index   24

Web Sites   24

Even at the age of two, Lois Lowry was interested in books! She was a very early reader, learning from her sister, who was three years older. When Lois went into first grade, they moved her up to third, so she was always the youngest in the class.

A Life in Fiction

Many of the books Lois Lowry has written are based on memories from her life. In her books Lois has brought to life some of the people, pets, places, and events of her lifetime. She has taken these **experiences** and turned them into wonderful, unforgettable stories of **fiction**. Lois has said the character of Anastasia's mother, Katherine, from her popular series Anastasia Krupnik, reminds her of herself. A friend's memories of war-torn Denmark **inspired** her book *Number the Stars*. Lois's first children's book, *A Summer to Die*, is based on the death of her sister, Helen.

Lois has said she never gets tired of writing about Anastasia Krupnik and her family from The Anastasia Series. At the end of the first book Anastasia's little brother Sam is born. Many of her readers liked Sam so much they asked Lois to create a series especially for him. Thus, the Sam Krupnik Series was born.

The Middle Child

Lois Lowry was born on March 20, 1937, in Honolulu, Hawaii. She was the second child of Katherine and Robert Hammersberg. Her father was an army dentist and officer. Her older sister, Helen, often acted as a little mother. She made sure that Lois did what she was told. Her younger brother, Jon, is almost six years younger than Lois. He was the baby of the family.

Lois spent much of her time reading. She imagined that she lived in the worlds where the books took her. She was a shy child who was neither **adventurous** nor **rebellious**.

However, she was very curious about the world. Lois found some answers to her curiosity in books.

Lois (right) is shown here with her older sister and baby brother. Lois feels that she was lucky being the middle child. Not being either the dependable oldest child or the youngest gave her the freedom to go off on her own.

Pictured here is Lois's grandparents' house, which inspired Autumn Street. The book is about a girl who lives with her grandfather when her father leaves to fight in World War II.

A Childhood in Carlisle

In 1942, during **World War II**, Lois's father left to serve overseas. Five-year-old Lois, her mother, and her sister moved to Carlisle, Pennsylvania. They went to live with her mother's parents. Her brother was born months after they arrived there.

For the next six years, Lois settled into life in Carlisle. There she attended school and made friends. Her grandparents lived in a large house. There were maids, a special porch for sleeping on hot summer nights, and a library with walls full of books. The house, the street, and the neighbors served as an inspiration for her book *Autumn Street*. Lois wrote that book in 1980.

Dogs have always been much-loved members of Lois Lowry's family. Her first dog was an Airedale puppy named Punky. When the dog bit her little brother, Lois's mother said they had to get rid of him. Seven-year-old Lois thought she meant little Jon and said, "okay." Of course her mother meant Punky, not the baby.

Life in Tokyo

When the war was over, Lois's family moved to Tokyo, Japan, in 1948. Her father, who was an army officer, was stationed there. The family lived with other American citizens in a little village called Washington Heights. It was in the center of Tokyo. The small village had its own church, schools, movie theater, and library. Lois attended junior high school in Tokyo, traveling by bus each day from Washington Heights. Lois was curious about Tokyo beyond her safe American community. She wanted to find out what lay beyond the village. Many times she went **exploring** without her parents' knowledge. Lois rode her bicycle to a part of Tokyo called Shibuya. It was an area full of life, and Lois loved it.

> "Days went by, and weeks. Jonas learned, through the memories, the names of colors; and now he began to see them all, in his ordinary life (though he knew it was ordinary no longer, and would never be again)."
> —from p. 97 of The Giver

Here Lois is in Japanese dress at age 12. When Lois remembers her time in Tokyo, she especially remembers the smells, sounds, and colors of Shibuya.

In 1958, Lois and Donald's daughter Alix (kneeling) was born. Their son Grey (standing left), daughter Kristin (standing right), and son Benjamin (on Lois's lap) were born during the first six years of the Lowrys' marriage. This picture was taken in 1963.

Marriage and a Family

In 1951, the family moved again, this time to New York City. Here Lois attended and **graduated** from a small private girls' high school in 1954. That fall Lois entered Brown University in Providence, Rhode Island. She had dreams of earning a college **degree** and of becoming a **novelist**.

In college Lois met Donald Grey Lowry. By 1956 Donald was a young officer in the U.S. Navy, and Lois dropped out of college to marry him. Like her parents and many military families, the Lowrys made many moves. They lived on navy bases in California, Connecticut, Florida, and South Carolina. During this time Lois and Donald had four children.

Lois had finished two years of college when she married at the early age of 19. She says that up until that time she had never even cooked a meal or done any laundry. Two years later she was busy looking after her first baby!

First Children's Book

The family moved to a farmhouse in Maine in 1963. Lois later decided to go back to college. She earned her college degree from the University of Southern Maine in 1973. It was around this time that she also began to write short fiction stories for magazines.

An **editor** at the Houghton Mifflin **publishing** company noticed her stories and liked them. The editor asked Lois if she had thought about writing a book for children. In 1976, Lois began work on her first children's novel, *A Summer to Die*. In the book a young girl named Meg has to deal with her older sister's illness and death. This was something Lois had experienced in 1962 with the loss of her own sister.

"The night breeze moved the dark curtains at the open windows. Outside, she knew, the sky was speckled with stars. How could anyone number them one by one, as the psalm said? There were too many. The sky was too big."
—from p. 87 of Number the Stars

This picture shows Lois in 1973, around the time she first started writing fiction.

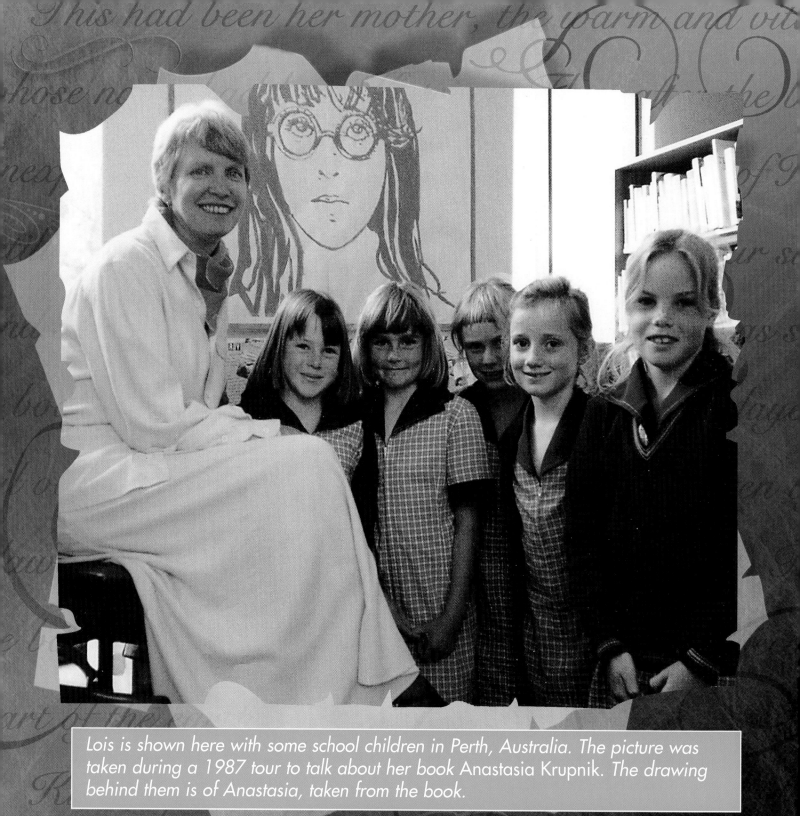

Lois is shown here with some school children in Perth, Australia. The picture was taken during a 1987 tour to talk about her book Anastasia Krupnik. The drawing behind them is of Anastasia, taken from the book.

Making Life Changes

At the age of 40, Lois made many changes in her life. She left her marriage of 21 years when she divorced Donald. Her children, ages 15, 16, 18, and 19, divided their time between their parents. Two years later Lois moved to Boston, Massachusetts, and settled into a small three-room apartment. The apartment was a lot smaller than the big farmhouse in Maine where she had raised her family. However, it was just the right size for her to continue her writing. That year her book *A Summer to Die* received the International Reading Association **Award**. It also got an award from the American Library Association. Lois also began work on a book called *Anastasia Krupnik* about a 10-year-old girl.

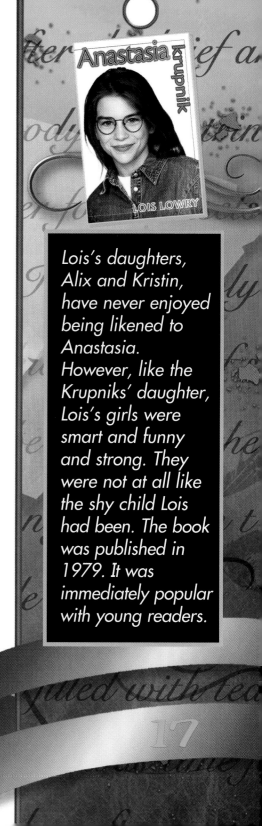

Lois's daughters, Alix and Kristin, have never enjoyed being likened to Anastasia. However, like the Krupniks' daughter, Lois's girls were smart and funny and strong. They were not at all like the shy child Lois had been. The book was published in 1979. It was immediately popular with young readers.

The Highest Award

Lois published *Number the Stars* in 1989. It tells the story of Annemarie, a 10-year-old Danish girl. Annemarie saves her Jewish friend Ellen and her family from being caught and killed by **Nazi** soldiers. *Number the Stars* shows how ordinary people, even a young child, can stand up to evil. The book won the 1990 Newbery Medal. Four years later Lois won the 1994 Newbery Medal for her book *The Giver*. The novel is about a **futuristic** world in which people have forgotten the experience of pain, hunger, and war. At the same time, people are no longer able to see color or experience other joys of life. Lois has said both books explore the bravery in taking **risks**.

Here Lois is receiving the Boston Public Library Junior Literary Lights Award from a young Boston student. Inset: The covers of the books that receive the Newbery award are stamped with a gold-colored medal. Here you can see the Newbery stamp on the 1990 winner, Number the Stars.

This recent picture shows Lois at her desk where she does all her writing.

A Writer's Life

Today Lois lives in Cambridge, Massachusetts, in a home filled with books. There is certain to be a dog somewhere in the house. Perhaps it will be sleeping on her kitchen floor. She has had a longtime friendship with a man named Martin. Lois and Martin own a farmhouse in Maine where they spend their weekends. She enjoys having her children and grandchildren visit her there.

Lois begins her mornings at 8:00 A.M. sitting in front of her computer. She says it takes about six months to write one of her books for children and young adults. Lois Lowry says she has never wanted to do anything but write. Children everywhere who love reading are very lucky for that.

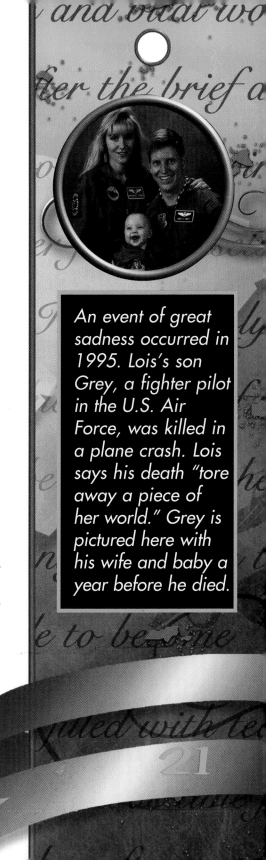

An event of great sadness occurred in 1995. Lois's son Grey, a fighter pilot in the U.S. Air Force, was killed in a plane crash. Lois says his death "tore away a piece of her world." Grey is pictured here with his wife and baby a year before he died.

21

In Her Own Words

How do you think of titles for your books?

I always think of the title last. I reread the book after I have written it, and I think, what is this book about? Then I try to think of a short phrase that will convey something of that. Sometimes I actually find the phrase within the book. That's where the title *Number the Stars* came from.

What is your favorite book?

Two of my favorites of my own books are *Rabble Starkey* and *Autumn Street*.

What was your favorite book as a child?

I had a lot of favorite books when I was young, but I think my all-time most favorite was *The Yearling* by Marjorie Kinnan Rawlings.

How can I get to be a writer?

Read a lot. I mean really a lot. When you're reading think about how the author did things. How did the author create a character who is interesting? Read the first paragraph of *Anastasia Krupnik* or the first two pages of *Gooney Bird Greene*, and see if you can figure out how I created those two characters.

Glossary

adventurous (ad-VEN-cher-us) Willing to risk danger to have new adventures.

award (uh-WORD) Something that is given after careful thought.

degree (duh-GREE) A title given to a person who has finished a course of study.

editor (EH-dih-ter) The person who corrects mistakes, checks facts, and decides what will be printed in a newspaper, book, or magazine.

experiences (ik-SPEER-ee-ents-iz) Events that a person has taken part in.

exploring (ek-SPLOR-ing) Traveling over little-known land.

fiction (FIK-shun) Stories that tell about people and events that are not real.

futuristic (fyoo-chuh-RIS-tik) Relating to a time to come.

graduated (GRA-joo-wayt-ed) To have finished a course of school.

inspired (in-SPYRD) Filled with excitement about something.

Nazi (NOT-see) Having to do with a member of the German army during World War II under the leadership Adolf Hitler.

novelist (NOV-list) A person who writes books about made-up people and events.

publishing (PUB-lish-ing) Having to do with printing matter people can read.

rebellious (ruh-BEL-yus) Having to do with fighting against one's parents or other people in authority.

risks (RISKS) Chances of loss or harm.

World War II (WURLD WOR TOO) A war fought by the United States, Great Britain, France, and the Soviet Union against Germany, Japan, and Italy from 1939 to 1945.

23

Index

A

American Library
    Association, 17
Anastasia Krupnik,
    5, 17
Autumn Street, 9

C

Cambridge,
    Massachusetts,
    21
Carlisle,
    Pennsylvania, 9

G

Giver, The, 18

H

Hammersberg,
    Katherine
    (mother), 6, 9
Hammersberg,
    Robert (father),
    6, 10

I

International
    Reading
    Association
    Award, 17

L

Lowry, Donald
    Grey, 13, 17

N

New York City,
    New York, 13
Newbery Medal,
    18
Number the Stars,
    5, 18

S

Summer to Die, A,
    14, 17

T

Tokyo, Japan, 10

W

World War II, 9

Web Sites

Due to the changing nature of Internet links, PowerKids Press has developed an online list of Web sites related to the subject of this book. This site is updated regularly. Please use this link to access the list:
www.powerkidslinks.com/aa/loislowry/